To our Neighbors
We are blessed to know
you & have you as our
neighbors. Thank you for sharing
your family with Morgen and
for supporting our family :)

Merry Christmas &
God bless you all!

2006   The Wohrlus :)

Published by Barbour Publishing, Inc., P.O. Box 719, Uhrichsville, Ohio 44683, www.barbourbooks.com

 Member of the
Evangelical Christian
Publishers Association

Printed in China.
5 4 3 2 1

The Birthday of a King

of a King

Lori Shankle

DayMaker
GREETING BOOKS

Jesus is Emmanuel—God with us!

Let us celebrate the awesome gift

that came to us that first Christmas

so long ago

when the King of kings was born.

CONTENTS

The Christmas season is one of wonder and magic for young and old alike. But, as E. B. White wrote, "To perceive Christmas through its wrapping becomes more difficult with every year." We get so caught up in, and often overwhelmed by, "the holiday season"—the preparation and planning, the decorations, the presents, the parties—that we forget the true reason for our celebration. The purpose of this time of year is to celebrate the birthday of a King—to remember who He is, why He came, and what He means to us.

1
the prophecy of his birth

From the moment that
Adam and Eve sinned in the garden,
God had a plan to forgive sin, redeem mankind,
and bring them back to Himself.

And the LORD God said unto the serpent,
Because thou hast done this, thou art
cursed. . .and I will put enmity between thee and the
woman, and between thy seed and her seed;
it shall bruise thy head, and thou shalt bruise his heel.

GENESIS 3:14–15

God's plan was not completely understood by men,
though Jesus' birth, life, death, resurrection, and future
reign were prophesied throughout the Old Testament,
thousands of years before He was born.
At the time of His birth, the Jewish leaders expected
an earthly king who would reign over them and free
them from the tyranny of Rome. Yet God's plan was so
much more—the birth of this one child has completely
changed the history of the world.

For unto us a child is born, unto us a son is given:
and the government shall be upon his shoulder:
and his name shall be called Wonderful, Counsellor,
The mighty God, The everlasting Father,
The Prince of Peace.

ISAIAH 9:6

But thou, Bethlehem Ephratah,

though thou be little among

the thousands of Judah, yet out of thee

shall he come forth unto me

that is to be ruler in Israel; whose goings

forth have been from of old, from everlasting.

MICAH 5:2

Therefore the Lord himself

shall give you a sign;

Behold, a virgin shall conceive,

and bear a son,

and shall call his name

Immanuel.

ISAIAH 7:14

O Come, O Come, Emmanuel

O come, O come, Emmanuel,
And ransom captive Israel,
That mourns in lonely exile here
Until the Son of God appear.

Rejoice! Rejoice! Emmanuel
Shall come to thee, O Israel.

2

THE PREPARATION FOR HIS BIRTH

And in the sixth month the angel Gabriel

was sent from God unto a city of Galilee, named Nazareth,

to a virgin espoused to a man whose name was Joseph,

of the house of David;

and the virgin's name was Mary.

And the angel said unto her, Fear not, Mary:

for thou hast found favour with God.

And, behold, thou shalt conceive in thy womb,

and bring forth a son, and shalt call his name JESUS.

LUKE 1:26–27, 30–31

The Angel Gabriel

THE ANGEL GABRIEL FROM GOD
WAS SENT TO GALILEE,
UNTO A VIRGIN FAIR AND FREE,
WHOSE NAME WAS CALLED MARY.
AND WHEN THE ANGEL THITHER CAME,
HE FELL DOWN ON HIS KNEE,
AND LOOKING UP IN THE VIRGIN'S FACE,
HE SAID, "ALL HAIL, MARY."

THEN SING WE ALL, BOTH GREAT AND SMALL,
NOWELL, NOWELL, NOWELL;
WE MAY REJOICE TO HEAR THE VOICE,
OF THE ANGEL GABRIEL.

"MARY," HE SAID, "BE NOT AFRAID,
BUT DO BELIEVE IN ME:
THE POWER OF THE HOLY GHOST
SHALL OVERSHADOW THEE;
THOU SHALT CONCEIVE WITHOUT ANY GRIEF,
AS THE LORD TOLD UNTO ME;
GOD'S OWN DEAR SON FROM HEAVEN SHALL COME,
AND SHALL BE BORN OF THEE."

TRADITIONAL ENGLISH CAROL

And Joseph also went up
from Galilee, out of the city
of Nazareth, into Judaea, unto
the city of David, which is called
Bethlehem; (because he was of
the house and lineage of David:)
to be taxed with Mary his espoused
wife, being great with child.

LUKE 2:4–5

No Room in the Inn

When Caesar Augustus had raised a taxation,
    He assessed all the people that dwelt in the nation;
The Jews at that time, being under Rome's sway,
    Appeared in the city their tribute to pay.

Then Joseph and Mary, who from David did spring,
    Went up to the city of David, their king;
And there, being entered, cold welcome they find:
    From the rich to the poor, they are mostly unkind.

Good Joseph was troubled, but most for his dear,

    For her blessed burden whose time now drew near;

His heart with true sorrow was sorely afflicted

    That his virgin spouse was so rudely neglected.

O Bethlehem, Bethlehem, welcome this stranger

    That was born in a stable and laid in a manger;

For He is a physician to heal all our smarts:

    Come welcome, sweet Jesus, and lodge in our hearts.

TRADITIONAL ENGLISH CAROL

3

The Proclamation of His Birth

When God sent His Son to the world,
He did not make the announcement to
those whom we would expect.
Of all the noteworthy people who should have known
about the birth of a king, none were informed.
God knew that the birth of this King
would mean something completely different
than any before or after Him—
He would be a King for all people.
So He came in an unusual way.

The Birthday of a King

In the little village of Bethlehem,
There lay a Child one day;
And the sky was bright with a holy light
O'er the place where Jesus lay.

Alleluia! O how the angels sang.
Alleluia! How it rang!
And the sky was bright with a holy light
'Twas the birthday of a King.

'Twas a humble birthplace, but O how much
God gave to us that day,
From the manger bed what a path has led,
What a perfect, holy way.

WILLIAM H. NEIDLINGER

Behold the Great Creator Makes

Behold the great Creator makes
Himself a house of clay,
A robe of virgin flesh He takes
Which He will wear for ay.
Hark, hark, the wise eternal Word,
Like a weak infant cries!
In form of servant is the Lord,
And God in cradles lies.
This wonder struck the world amazed,
It shook the starry frame;
Squadrons of spirits stood and gazed,
Then down in troops they came.
Glad shepherds ran to view this sight;
A choir of angels sings,
And eastern sages with delight
Adore this King of kings.
Join then, all hearts that are not stone,
And all our voices prove,
To celebrate this holy One
The God of peace and love.

Thomas Pestel

When God proclaimed the birth of His Son to the
people of earth, He also chose to make the
announcement in an unusual way. The angels
of heaven appeared to one of the lowliest
groups of all—the shepherds who were
watching their sheep out in the fields.

And there were in the same country shepherds
abiding in the field, keeping watch over their flock
by night. And, lo, the angel of the Lord came upon them,
and the glory of the Lord shone round about them: and
they were sore afraid. And the angel said unto them,
Fear not: for, behold, I bring you good tidings of
great joy, which shall be to all people. For unto you
is born this day in the city of David
a Saviour, which is Christ the Lord.

LUKE 2:8–11

While by My Sheep I Watched at Night

While by my sheep I watched at night,
Glad tidings brought an angel bright.
How great my joy, great my joy.
Joy, joy, joy! Joy, joy, joy!
Praise we the Lord in heaven on high.
Praise we the Lord in heaven on high.

There shall be born, so did he say,
In Bethlehem a Child today.

There shall He lie in manger mean,
Who shall redeem the world from sin.

Lord, evermore to me be nigh,
Then shall my heart be filled with joy!

OLD GERMAN CAROL

The First Noel

The first Noel
the angel did say,
Was to certain poor shepherds
in fields as they lay;
In fields where they lay
keeping their sheep
On a cold winter's night
that was so deep.

Noel, Noel, Noel, Noel,
Born is the King of Israel.

TRADITIONAL CAROL

Silent Night

Silent night, holy night!
Shepherds quake at the sight,
Glories stream from heaven afar,
Heav'nly hosts sing alleluia;
Christ the Saviour is born!
Christ the Saviour is born!

JOSEPH MOHR

And suddenly there was with the angel
a multitude of the heavenly host praising God, and saying,
Glory to God in the highest, and on earth
peace, good will toward men.

LUKE 2:13–14

Angels We Have Heard on High

Angels we have heard on high,
Sweetly singing o'er the plains;
And the mountains in reply
Echoing their joyous strains

Gloria in excelsis Deo,
Gloria in excelsis Deo.

TRADITIONAL FRENCH CAROL

Angels, from the Realms of Glory

Angels, from the realms of glory,
Wing your flight o'er all the earth;
Ye who sang creation's story,
Now proclaim Messiah's birth:
Come and worship, Come and worship,
Worship Christ, the newborn King!

Shepherds, in the fields abiding,
Watching o'er your flocks by night,
God with man is now residing,
Yonder shines the infant Light:
Come and worship, Come and worship,
Worship Christ, the newborn King!

JAMES MONTGOMERY

The birth of the King of kings was also "announced" to Gentile astrologers who watched the stars in the sky. They obviously saw something miraculous, which motivated them to travel a far distance to worship this King and bring Him gifts!

Now when Jesus was born in Bethlehem of Judaea in the days of Herod the king, behold, there came wise men from the east to Jerusalem, saying, Where is he that is born King of the Jews? for we have seen his star in the east, and are come to worship him. . . and, lo, the star, which they saw in the east, went before them, till it came and stood over where the young child was. When they saw the star, they rejoiced with exceeding great joy. And when they were come into the house, they saw the young child with Mary his mother, and fell down, and worshipped him: and when they had opened their treasures, they presented unto him gifts; gold, and frankincense and myrrh.

MATTHEW 2:1–2, 9–11

We Three Kings of Orient Are

We three kings of Orient are,
Bearing gifts we traverse afar,
Field and fountain, moor and mountain,
Following yonder star.

O star of wonder, star of night,
Star with royal beauty bright,
Westward leading, still proceeding,
Guide us to thy perfect light.

JOHN HENRY HOPKINS, JR.

The Three Kings

Three Kings came riding from far away,
Melchior and Gaspar and Baltasar;
Three Wise Men out of the East were they,
And they traveled by night and they slept by day,
For their guide was a beautiful, wonderful star.

The star was so beautiful, large and clear,
That all the other stars of the sky
Became a white mist in the atmosphere;
And by this they knew that the coming was near
Of the Prince foretold in the prophecy.

Three caskets they bore on their saddle-bows,
Three caskets of gold with golden keys;
Their robes were of crimson silk, with rows
Of bells and pomegranates and furbelows,
Their turbans like blossoming almond-trees.

And so the Three Kings rode into the West,
Through the dusk of night over hill and dell,
And sometimes they nodded with beard on breast,
And sometimes talked, as they paused to rest,
With the people they met at some wayside well.

"Of the Child that is born," said Baltasar,
"Good people, I pray you, tell us the news;
For we in the East have seen his star,
And have ridden fast, and have ridden far,
To find and worship the King of the Jews."

And the people answered, "You ask in vain;
We know of no king but Herod the Great!"
They thought the Wise Men were men insane,
As they spurred their horses across the plain
Like riders in haste who cannot wait.

And when they came to Jerusalem,
Herod the Great, who had heard this thing,
Sent for the Wise Men and questioned them;
And said, "Go down unto Bethlehem,
And bring me tidings of this new king."

So they rode away, and the star stood still,
The only one in the gray of morn;
Yes, it stopped, it stood still of its own free will,
Right over Bethlehem on the hill,
The city of David where Christ was born.

And the Three Kings rode through the gate and the guard,
Through the silent street, till their horses turned
And neighed as they entered the great inn-yard;
But the windows were closed, and the doors were barred,
And only a light in the stable burned.

And cradled there in the scented hay,
In the air made sweet by the breath of kine,
The little Child in the manger lay,
The Child that would be King one day
Of a kingdom not human, but divine.

His mother, Mary of Nazareth,
Sat watching beside his place of rest,
Watching the even flow of his breath,
For the joy of life and the terror of death
Were mingled together in her breast.

They laid their offerings at his feet:
The gold was their tribute to a King;
The frankincense, with its odor sweet,
Was for the Priest, the Paraclete;
The myrrh for the body's burying.

And the mother wondered and bowed her head,
And sat as still as a statue of stone;
Her heart was troubled yet comforted,
Remembering what the angel had said
Of an endless reign and of David's throne.

Then the Kings rode out of the city gate,
With a clatter of hoofs in proud array;
But they went not back to Herod the Great,
For they knew his malice and feared his hate,
And returned to their homes by another way.

Henry Wadsworth Longfellow

The first wise men gave
Christ treasures from their
kingdoms. Today's wise men
give the treasure of their hearts.

Holley Armstrong

4

THE PURPOSE OF HIS BIRTH

JESUS. . .

Through His incarnation we came face-to-face with mercy.

Through His life we came to know the heart of God.

Through His resurrection we came to experience the joy of salvation.

AUTHOR UNKNOWN

FOR THE SON OF MAN IS COME TO
SEEK AND TO SAVE THAT WHICH WAS LOST.

LUKE 19:10

*But as many as received him, to them
gave he power to become the sons of God,
even to them that believe on his name.*

JOHN 1:12

The Saviour's Work

The Babe in Bethlehem's manger laid
In humble form so low;
By wondering angels is surveyed
Through all His scenes of woe.

Nowell, Nowell,
now sing a Saviour's birth,
All hail His coming down to earth
Who raises us to Heaven!

A Saviour! Sinners all around
Sing, shout the wondrous word;
Let every bosom hail the sound,
A Saviour! Christ the Lord.

For not to sit on David's throne
With worldly pomp and joy,
He came on earth for sin to atone,
And Satan to destroy.

To preach the word of life divine,
And feed with living bread,
To heal the sick with hand benign
And raise to life the dead.

He preached, He suffered, bled and died
Uplift 'twixt earth and skies;
In sinners stead was crucified,
For a sin a sacrifice.

TRADITIONAL ENGLISH CAROL

The Holly and the Ivy

The Holly and the Ivy,
When they are both full grown
Of all the trees are in the wood,
The Holly bears the crown.

O the rising of the sun,
And the running of the deer,
The playing of the merry organ,
Sweet singing in the choir.

The Holly bears a blossom
As white as any flower;
And Mary bore sweet Jesus Christ
To be our sweet Saviour.

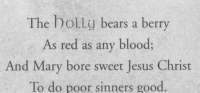

The Holly bears a berry
As red as any blood;
And Mary bore sweet Jesus Christ
To do poor sinners good.

The Holly bears a prickle
As sharp as any thorn;
And Mary bore sweet Jesus Christ
On Christmas in the morn.

The Holly bears a bark
As bitter as any gall;
And Mary bore sweet Jesus Christ
For to redeem us all.

The Holly and the Ivy
Now both are full well grown:
Of all the trees are in the wood
The Holly bears the crown.

TRADITIONAL ENGLISH CAROL

HARK! THE HERALD ANGELS SING

Hark! The herald angels sing,
"Glory to the newborn King;
Peace on earth, and mercy mild,
God and sinners reconciled!"

CHARLES WESLEY

What Child Is This?

The King of kings salvation brings,
Let loving hearts enthrone Him.

WILLIAM CHATTERTON DIX

I am come that they might have life,
and that they might have it
more abundantly.

JOHN 10:10

The Spirit of the Lord is upon me, because
he hath anointed me to preach the gospel to
the poor; he hath sent me to heal the brokenhearted,
to preach deliverance to the captives, and
recovering of sight to the blind, to set at
liberty them that are bruised, to preach
the acceptable year of the Lord.

LUKE 4:18–19

For when we were yet without strength, in
due time Christ died for the ungodly. But God
commendeth his love toward us, in that, while we
were yet sinners, Christ died for us.

ROMANS 5:6, 8

ONE SOLITARY LIFE

He was born in an obscure village,
the child of a peasant woman.
He grew up in still another village,
where he worked in a carpenter
shop until he was thirty.

Then for three years he was an
itinerant preacher.
He never wrote a book.
He never held an office.
He never had a family or
owned a house.
He didn't go to college.
He never visited a big city.
He never traveled two hundred miles
from the place where he was born.
He did none of the things one
usually associates with greatness.
He had no credentials but himself.

He was only thirty-three when the
tide of public opinion turned against him.
His friends ran away.
He was turned over to his enemies
and went through a mockery of a trial.
He was nailed to a cross between two thieves.
While he was dying, his executioners gambled for
his clothing, the only property he had on earth.

When he was dead, he was laid in a
borrowed grave through the pity of a friend.

Nineteen centuries have come and gone, and
today he is the central figure of the human
race and the leader of mankind's progress.
All the armies that ever marched, all the navies
that ever sailed, all the parliaments that ever sat,
all the kings that ever reigned, put together,
have not affected the life of man on this earth as
much as that ONE SOLITARY LIFE.

DR. JAMES ALLEN

The birth of the baby Jesus stands
as the most significant event in all history,
because it has meant the pouring into a sick
world of the healing medicine of love which
has transformed all manner of hearts for
almost two thousand years.

GEORGE MATTHEW ADAMS

What can I give Him,
Poor as I am?
If I were a shepherd
I would bring him a lamb—
If I were a wise man
I would do my part—
Yet what I can, I give Him,
Give my heart.

CHRISTINA ROSSETTI